Hidden in the Sands
Uncovering Qatar's Past

Frances Gillespie
Faisal Abdulla Al-Naimi

Consultant: Dr Richard Cuttler

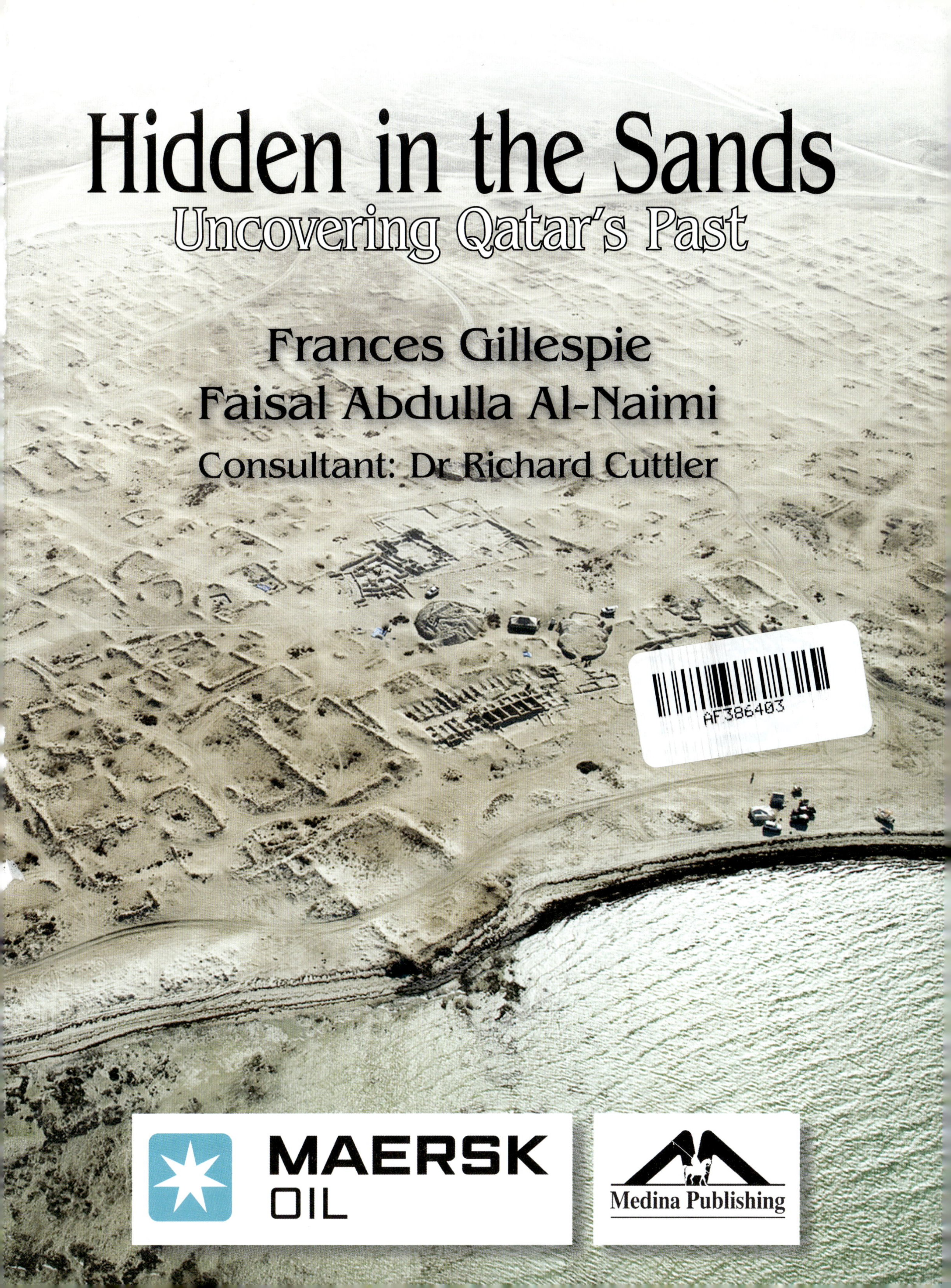

Acknowledgements

The publication of this book and the launch of its linked website (www.HiddenInTheSands.com) would not have been possible without the generous sponsorship of Maersk Oil (Qatar). Maersk Oil has provided me with invaluable assistance on cultural and environmental projects since 1997, and my debt to the company is immense.

Faisal Abdulla Al-Naimi, Head of Antiquities at the Qatar Museums Authority (QMA), has offered constant assistance and considered advice. Without his support and experience this book would not have been possible. This is most gratefully acknowledged, and his name appears as co-author to reflect this contribution.

Dr Richard Cuttler, Senior Research Fellow at the University of Birmingham and Director of the Qatar National Historic Environment Record (QNHER), kindly agreed to act as consultant for the book and has been a pillar of support, checking and correcting texts, offering advice, information, sourcing suitable photographs, and providing the maps showing the inundation of the Arabian Gulf. Dr Cuttler's colleagues Dr Emma Tetlow, Palaeoenvironmental Specialist, and Liam Delaney, QNHER Project Officer, provided the map of Qatar at the front of the book, and have also been most supportive.

Dr Georg Gerster, veteran aerial photographer of major archaeological and cultural sites worldwide, generously allowed the use of his photographs taken in Qatar.

Two experts on the ancient production of purple dye from molluscs, Dr Rolf Haubrichs and Inge Boesken Kanold, visited Qatar in 2012 and kindly supplied photographs and information.

Dr Flemming Højlund, Head of the Oriental Department at Moesgård Museum in Denmark, and his colleague Ulrik Høj Johnsen, the curator of the museum's ethnographical collection, offered valuable advice and gave permission to reproduce the photographs taken in 1959 of the bedu in Qatar by Prof. Klaus Ferdinand and Jette Bang.

Archaeologists from the various expeditions working in Qatar, either at the present time or in the past, have been overwhelmingly generous with information, supplying images and checking texts relating to sites on which they worked. They include, in addition to Dr Cuttler, Dr Ingolf Thuesen and Dr Alan Walmsley, Directors of the Qatar Islamic Archaeology and Heritage Project (QIAH) currently excavating at Al Zubara, and their colleagues Dr Tobias Richter, Dr Anna Razeto and Sandra Rosenthal. Dr Andrew Petersen, Director of a team from the University of Wales which is also part of QIAH, was most helpful with photographs from two other Islamic coastal sites covered in this book. Mr Anthony Grey, working as an independent consultant on ceramics with the QIAH, was endlessly kind in identifying not only ceramics from the sites with which he was involved but other sites as well. Dr Alexandrine Guerin, Director of the Mission Archéologique Française à Qatar, the most recent of the many teams to excavate at Murwab, and Dr Juergen Schreiber, now based in Munich as an independent consultant, kindly sent photographs and information.

I felt that it was important to include a chapter on conservation in order to show the whole archaeological process, from the discovery of objects to their eventual display in a museum. Lisa Usman, formerly chief conservator at the Museum of Islamic Art (MIA) in Doha, acted as consultant and supplied much of the information for Chapter 15. Conservators Susan Rees of the MIA, Valerie Free of the National Museum of Qatar (NMoQ) and visiting conservation consultant Hiroko Kariya, facilitated access to their laboratories for photographs to be taken, and supplied additional images.

Pearls and pearling experts Dr Hubert Bari, Director of the Qatar Pearl and Jewellery Museum and Dr Robert Carter, Senior Lecturer in Archaeology at the Qatar campus of University College London, generously allowed me to reproduce photographs in Chapter 12 that first appeared in their own superb publications.

Robert Jackson, a history teacher based in Oman, provided the splendid photograph of the replica ship *Jewel of Muscat* in full sail, which appears in the chapter on The Golden Age.

Amen Deeban, a photographer based at the MIA, supplied copies of the many images of artefacts taken for Heritage without Borders: the 3rd Joint GCC Archaeology Exhibition, held in Doha in 2011.

Staff at the Ministry of Culture, Arts and Heritage were most helpful in tracking down a photograph I needed.

Staff members from the Department of Antiquities most willingly helped to locate photographs taken by previous archaeological teams working in Qatar, and Meghan Magee, Senior Registrar with the NMoQ, readily provided information.

Deep personal gratitude is owed to my husband David Gillespie for his loving support throughout the production of the book, acting as photographer when needed, accompanying me to sites at weekends and tolerating the inundation of our home computer with hundreds of communications between the publishers and me as the book took shape.

Last but not least, my thanks go to our creative and talented illustrator, Norman MacDonald, and my wonderful publishers at Medina, Kitty Carruthers, with her flair for attractive and interesting design, and Peter Harrigan, who shares with me a love of Arabia and 'all things archaeological'.

Frances Gillespie
Doha 2013

Foreword

Our Qatari identity and shared past are important if we are to truly understand the vision of where we are going. The archaeological studies that continue to reveal Qatar's past have been carried out for over half a century. Modern archaeology is helping us to discover and learn about both the historic and prehistoric past, and today Qatar has some of the most experienced archaeologists in the world excavating and studying our rich sites.

In Qatar there are archaeological treasures both on land and underwater. As the writers of this book explain, thousands of years ago the Arabian Gulf was part of a huge river valley with human settlements. So now the sea bed, from where Maersk Oil Qatar – in close partnership with Qatar Petroleum – has been producing oil for nearly 20 years, is also the site of exciting archaeological discoveries that tell us about our past. As an international organisation we have always considered it our responsibility to make a positive and meaningful contribution to the communities in which we live, work and operate. In Qatar, Maersk Oil fully supports the Qatar National Vision 2030. One element of this support is delivered through our social investment programme, 'Action for Qatar'. Helping to inform Qataris, our foreign guests and many visitors about our past is an important element of the education pillar of our social investment programme, and by supporting this book and its linked website we hope to contribute to that. We are also sponsoring the construction of a temporary exhibition building at the unique historic site of the pearl trading town at

Al Zubara and funding an educational programme promoting better understanding of the history of the ancient town, thought to be the only complete historical pearling settlement in the Arabian Gulf.

The story of Al Zubara is told in this book, along with chapters on mysterious rock carvings, stone tools, pearling, ancient burial sites and our heritage and past way of life, both at sea and on land. What we learn is brought to life by many photographs and beautiful illustrations which vividly evoke the past. This book and the website are not just about our past but also tell us how archaeologists work and also how they help to conserve and preserve our past for the future.

As a Qatari with a leading role at Maersk Oil Qatar, I am proud to introduce this book that reveals our rich past and thank the authors for telling this important story.

Faisal bin Fahad Al-Thani
Deputy Managing Director
Maersk Oil Qatar

Qalaat Al Ruwaida
Jabal Fraiha
Al Zubara
Ras Eshairiq
Lisha
Al Rubaiqa
Wadi Al Debaiaan
Murwab
Umm Al Maa
Fuwairit
Jabal Al Jassasiya
Al Huwaila
Jazirat Bin Ghannam
Al Khor
Dukhan
Al Mazrouah
Al Da'asa
DOHA
QATAR
N
W
E
S
0 4 8 16 24 32 40
Kilometers

Contents

ARCHAEOLOGY IN QATAR

Where does all the information in this book come from?

There are many history books about Qatar and the countries around the Arabian Gulf and written records that provide us with fascinating accounts of daily life in years gone by. But writing was invented less than six thousand years ago, and so for anything earlier we can only rely on evidence on or below the ground. The finding, study and interpretation of this evidence is known as archaeology. It is a way of travelling back through time to discover how our ancestors lived, and much that we learn about the past comes from the work of archaeologists.

Archaeologists also record Qatar's past underwater!

What do archaeologists do?

Everyone knows that archaeologists dig! It's true that digging is still an important part of archaeology, but nowadays science is as much a part of archaeology as are spades and trowels. Archaeologists can spend as much time in a laboratory as on a site. They peer through microscopes to see the tiny flecks in a bit of pottery that can tell them where and when it was made, or the fibres in a scrap of cloth to see what it was made of and what technique the weaver used. They analyse and scientifically test human remains such as teeth and bones to reveal not only how long ago a person lived, but where he or she was born and brought up, what kind of diet they had, and what diseases they suffered from.

Faisal Al-Naimi discusses a find with Dr Alan Walmsley, director of excavations at Al Zubara

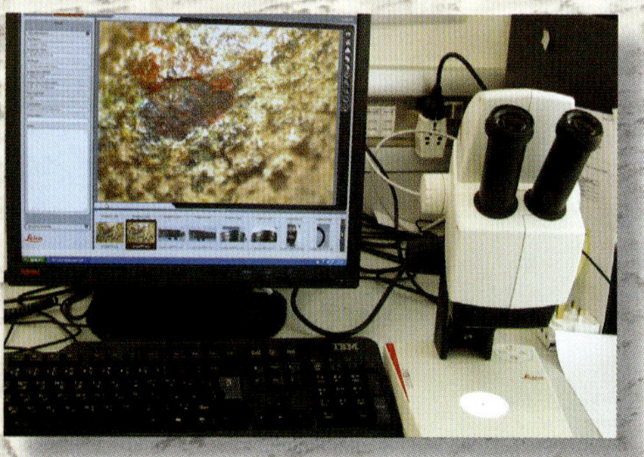

A tiny fragment of metal is being examined through a binocular microscope connected to a computer

Trash or treasure

The dark layers are the remains of a 5000-year old rubbish heap at Wadi Al Debaiaan

Some people imagine that archaeologists have a glamorous job, searching for fabulous treasure like Howard Carter, the famous discoverer of Tutankhamun's tomb in Egypt. But archaeology isn't always like that. It's true they sometimes strike gold, but very, very rarely. An archaeologist's idea of treasure is often a rubbish heap, from which they can tell more about the lifestyle of a people, what they and wore and worked at, than any amount of gold coins. Archaeologists work rather like detectives at a crime scene, piecing together tiny bits of evidence from a site, to work out what was going on there hundreds or even thousands of years ago. Everything is carefully drawn and recorded.

Archaeologists classify objects that they find into two basic groups: organic and inorganic. Organic means that they have come from what was once a living organism. This includes wood and charcoal, bone, leather and textiles and also such tiny objects as snail shells and the wing cases of beetles, or even seeds and pollen from plants.

By studying the remains of plants and insects, environmental archaeologists can understand what vegetation was growing thousands of years ago, what the climate was like and what kind of environment people were living in at the time. Organic remains can be tested by scientists in a laboratory to give an approximate date. Land snails, for example, prefer very specific habitats, so their remains give clues about the environment they lived in.

Inorganic remains include objects made of metal and stone, and glass and pottery. They cannot be laboratory tested for a date, although analysis of the substance they are made from can often identify the source of the stone or clay. Pottery styles change only slowly, and experts on Middle Eastern pottery can examine a fragment of pot and usually tell where and when it was made.

Because archaeologists study such a vast span of time they divide it into periods. Prehistory, the time before written records, is divided into the Stone Age, the Bronze Age and the Iron Age, named after the main materials people used to make tools and other objects during these periods.

The remains of a pearl merchant's wooden box found at Al Zubara

Neolithic flint tools

Stone Age — Palaeolithic, Mesolithic, Neolithic

Bronze Age — Iron Age

Islamic Golden Age — Hijrah calendar begins, Mediaeval, Modern

12000 11000 10000 9000 8000 7000 6000 5000 4000 3000 2000 1000 CE 622 1000 2000

When did it all begin?

Archaeology in Qatar really began in the 1950s, when teams of archaeologists arrived, first from Denmark and later from Britain and France, to work with their Qatari colleagues on sites as old as 8,000 years and as recent as 200. When the Qatar National Museum was opened in 1975 in a former palace it had a special display of objects from these sites.

How does the past get under the ground?

Sometimes objects are placed in the ground deliberately. Before the coming of Christianity and Islam, people often buried objects with their dead, to help them in their next life. A man might be buried with his sword or his dagger, a woman with her favourite necklace or a comb, and a child with a toy. Often a cairn, a mound of stones, was built over the grave. Very few burials of this kind in Qatar have survived intact: the possibility that valuable objects might lie under a cairn was just too tempting for ancient grave-robbers!

More often broken bits of pottery, or the remains of stone tools or buildings, simply get covered by drifting soil or sand, or by sediment carried by flash floods or rivers. Buildings fall down and new ones are constructed on top of the ruins. In Qatar, where the climate is very dry and there is not a lot of surface soil, objects are not often buried very deeply, and sometimes not at all: the first archaeologists in Qatar, in the 1950s, walked around collecting beautifully-made stone tools they found on the surface of the ground. These tools are not always found where they were dropped by the people who used them: the *shamal* wind scatters small objects far and wide across the desert floor.

The first Qatar National Museum was opened in a former palace in 1975. It will soon be surrounded by a stunning new building inspired by the shape of a desert rose

HOW ARCHAEOLOGISTS WORK

Bird's Eye View

When man first took to the air, first in balloons and then in aeroplanes, it opened up a whole new world for archaeologists. From above, it's possible to see all kinds of changes in the landscape that can't be seen from the ground. More recently, images taken from satellites have also helped locate new sites. These photos can be pieced together like a jigsaw to form 'photo-mosaics' and linked to national grid co-ordinates. They can then be accurately placed on a map.

The Right Tool for the Job

New technical equipment is constantly being invented which assists the work of archaeologists, but simple diamond-shaped trowels are still important basic tools. They are used to excavate layers or soil or sand, and the excavator can often feel the difference between the composition of the different layers. In Qatar the sand and soil is very dry so the excavator sometimes uses a brush to expose buried remains. For very fine and delicate work a dental pick can be useful.

If a site is covered with large amounts of modern debris a mechanical digger is used to clear it away. Shovels are used to remove more soil or sand and then the real work of the archaeologists can begin.

What's Down There?

Geophysical survey techniques collect large amounts of data. They allow archaeologists to know about deposits below the surface of an archaeological site without actually digging. Most instruments work by detecting physical or chemical changes in the ground. Maps produced by these instruments can be used as a guide for excavations, or indicate areas that should be avoided by future development.

Underground deposits conduct electricity in distinctive ways. A frame is used to insert two probes into the ground. An electrical resistance meter then measures the distance between the two probes. The wider the space between the probes, the deeper the measurement of resistance into the ground. If archaeological deposits are present then they may have a higher or lower electrical resistance than the surrounding geology. The data can be interpreted to make subsurface maps. Electrical resistance survey doesn't always work well in Qatar because electric currents travel much easier when the ground is moist, and much of the time the desert surface is very dry.

Past activities by ancient people, such as hearths and disturbed soil, can cause tiny changes in the earth's magnetic field. These can be detected using an instrument called a magnetometer. Readings of the earth's magnetic field are taken at regular intervals and are used to create a map of changes. On archaeological sites these often correspond to past activities on the site, especially those with areas of burning.

Write It Down!

It's important for archaeologists to record exactly where each object is found. Their location is recorded using survey equipment or on detailed plans. Each excavated layer is given a number and this number is given to all samples and objects taken from that layer. Later all the evidence from that layer can be assembled for study.

An archaeologist using a magnetometer to measure slight changes in the earth's magnetic field

Taking soil samples with an auger

Computers have revolutionised the recording and storage of archaeological information in the form of databases and digital archives. These can be combined with mapping, satellite imagery and information about the location of sites to form a Geographic Information System. A GIS allows the location of sites to be displayed, together with all kinds of information about the landscape, and this enables important decisions to be made about how future developments will affect archaeological sites.

The dating game

Objects such as coins of a known date can help to date a site. When a coin is found in a layer, unless the coin was deliberately buried we can be almost sure that the layer cannot be earlier than the date on the coin. Where deposits are found beneath a historically datable event, such as the construction of a fort, the deposit cannot date from before that period.

Carbon countdown

Radiocarbon dating is used by archaeologists working in Qatar and is only useful for dating organic remains. The radioactive forms of certain elements, such as carbon, are unstable and decay at a known rate, giving off energy and radiation. Radiocarbon dating is based on a radioactive form of carbon called carbon-14, or C14. By determining the amount of C14 remaining in a sample it is possible to determine its age and so the deposit with which it is associated.

Radiocarbon dates that account for both the amount of decay of C14 since the sample became buried, and for historic levels of C14 in the atmosphere, are known as calibrated radiocarbon dates.

Layer upon Layer

When several layers lie over each other on a site it is known as a stratigraphic sequence. The lower layers must have formed first so the most recent objects will be in the top layer. But sometimes postholes or rubbish pits have been dug into earlier layers and they in turn get covered with more layers! So dating the various layers can be a complicated business.

Searching for Shipwrecks

For thousands of years, before a rise in sea levels, the Arabian Gulf was a landscape occupied by ancient people. After sea levels rose the region became part of a major trade network, with goods passing by ship between Mesopotamia, in what is now Iraq, and India. Marine archaeologists believe that during thousands of years of trade some ships sank and now remain at the bottom of the Gulf.

Marine geophysicists use sonar instruments that send out sound pulses which reflect back from both the sea bed surface and beneath, to help them locate remains of submerged landscapes and ancient shipwrecks.

The maps of the sea bed and sediments immediately below can provide valuable clues and lead to exciting discoveries. Divers and cameras mounted on remote-controlled submarines can then descend to find out if they are archaeological sites or discover a shipwreck.

We can also learn more about the past environment by drilling cores of sediment out from the sea bed, which are then analysed. The presence of pollen, plant remains and minute organisms in the sediments can provide evidence of conditions in the past, and C14 analysis can provide dates for the ancient deposits that have been brought to the surface for investigation.

Recording underwater remains around Qatar's coast

Lots of things get buried in the same place. Usually, the deeper they are buried, the older they are

Recording a prehistoric burial cairn at Ras Eshairiq, north-west Qatar

THE FIRST PEOPLE

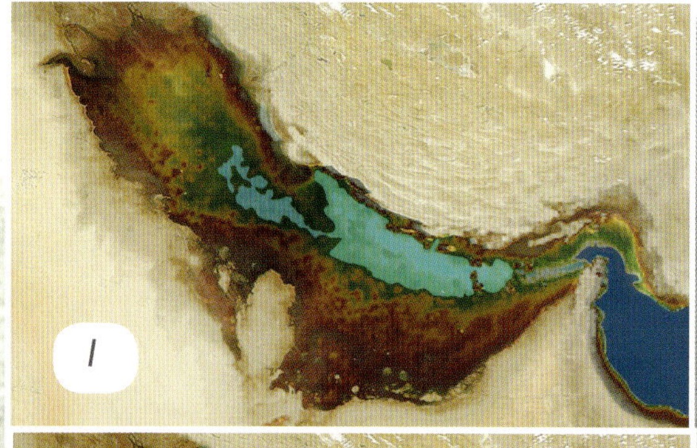

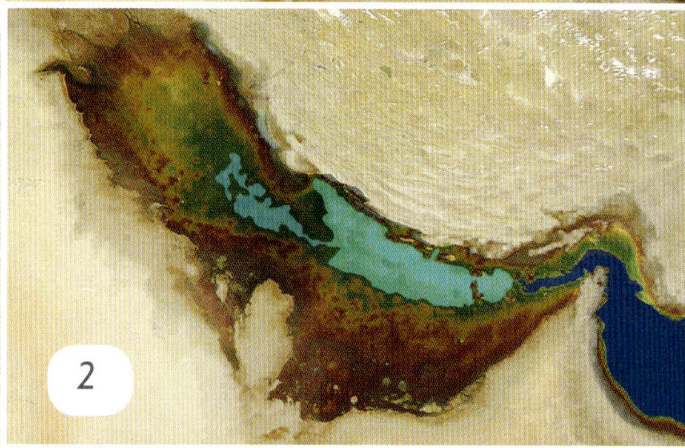

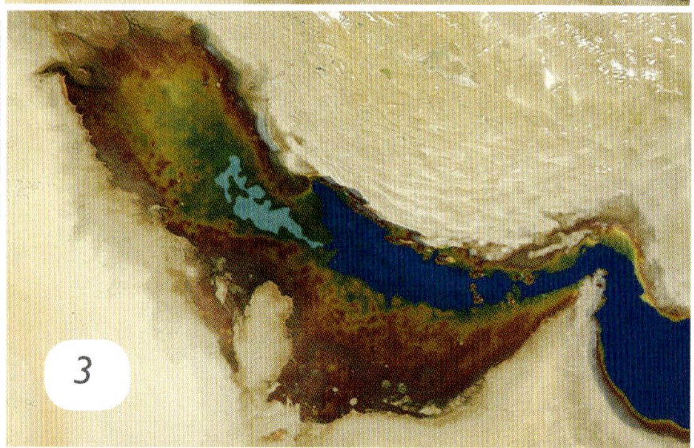

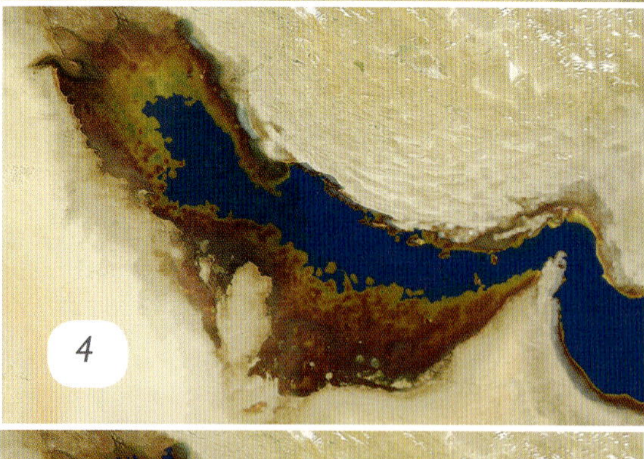

These images show how the Arabian Gulf gradually flooded:

1. 14,000 BP
2. 13,000 BP
3. 12,000 BP
4. 10,000 BP
5. 8,200 BP

When did humans first come to Qatar?

No one is quite sure of the answer to this question. But new discoveries are being made all the time which are changing our ideas and theories about the earliest people to live in Arabia.

The latest exciting archaeological discoveries point to the first migration of modern humans into Arabia taking place 106,000 years ago – some 50,000 years earlier than we first thought.

At that time the basin of the Arabian Gulf was dry, flat land, marshy in places, with an ancient, slow-moving river, the Shatt-Al-Arab, running along its length from what is now Iraq southwards towards the Strait of Hormuz. The present Tigris and Euphrates rivers in Iraq were among its tributaries.

Besides the great river there were two large lakes and a mosaic of springs, mangrove swamps and estuaries with thick beds of tall reeds with plenty of fish. During this period, Arabia's climate was wetter and the vegetation would have been green and lush, providing plentiful food for the animals and birds that were hunted. Because the land was flat the river ran slowly, depositing silt which created fertile land for growing crops. The people living beside the river and its tributaries may have built their houses of reeds, and they probably cultivated date palms, like the Marsh Arabs of Iraq today.

Nowadays the level of the aquifers – the water table beneath the peninsula of Qatar – has lowered because of the number of people drawing water from it, and the change to a more arid climate means that the aquifers are not being replenished by rainfall. But in those days plentiful fresh water was available from springs along the coast and even from beneath the sea.

Drowned lands

Around 15,000 years ago the last Ice Age drew to a close, and melting ice at the poles caused sea levels to rise. Gradually, the Gulf basin began to be inundated with sea water from the Indian Ocean through the Strait of Hormuz. This was no sudden flood; people did not become refugees overnight. But, little by little, fertile land disappeared beneath salty water. People would have been forced to move their camps away from the floor of the Gulf and onto higher ground. The highest sea level was reached about 7,500 years ago, and this may be the reason why so many remains of settlements along the present shores of the Gulf date to this time. Some of the coastal settlements had well-built houses of stone, and the inhabitants made beautifully-crafted tools of flint and imported finely-decorated pottery. There is evidence from the pottery, and from objects such as beads made of stone from Mesopotamia and eastern Turkey, that they were part of an established trading network.

Trading boats were made of bundles of reeds, water-proofed with a bitumen coating sourced from what is now Kuwait and Iraq. A small painted ceramic disc from this period, found on a site in Kuwait, shows a reed boat with a mast, and is the earliest known depiction of a boat in the Arabian Gulf. Reed-bundle boats were also used for fishing and pearling. People may have traded pearls, shell beads and dried fish in exchange for the pottery and other goods. Qatar lacks deposits of clay suitable for pottery-making, so all pottery had to be imported.

At the time these settlements were first built Qatar was almost an island, connected to the Arabian Peninsula by a narrow neck of land. The area around the Inland Sea that is now covered in giant sand dunes was once underwater! Since then the sea level relative to the land in the Gulf has dropped about two metres, leaving some of the remains on ancient shorelines which are now several kilometres inland from today's coastline.

When these early settlers lived in Qatar it was far greener than it is now. The north-west wind, the *shamal* which blows so strongly today, was weaker then and allowed the rain-bearing monsoon to reach Qatar from the south. There would have been fresh-water lakes and forests, more like the landscape of southern Oman today. But then the climate changed, the wind grew stronger and the monsoon no longer watered the landscape. Qatar became the desert that it is today.

The reed houses may have been similar to these from the northern Arabian Gulf

Neolithic mollusc shells pierced with holes for use as ornaments

Animals like the Arabian oryx were hunted for food

The 'Tigris', a replica reed boat built in 1977, sailed 6,800 km from Iraq down the Arabian Gulf and across the Indian Ocean to Africa

EARLY COASTAL SETTLEMENTS

In the 1970s an exciting discovery was made by archaeologists when they found fragments of painted pottery, known as Ubaid, on a site called Al Da'asa, south of Dukhan on the west coast.

The pottery is named after a site where it was first identified by archaeologists near the city of Ur in the ancient land of Mesopotamia, now part of Iraq. Al Da'asa was the first of the so-called 'Ubaid sites' in Qatar to be identified, and the finds provided more proof that these ancient people were trading by boat right up to the head of the Gulf and on waterways beyond.

The pottery dates to between 7000 and 6000 BP, and is light green or buff coloured, painted with attractive black geometric patterns. Pottery imported from so far away was valuable – one fragment of Ubaid pot shows signs of having been carefully repaired.

There were post holes which may show where tents or possibly palm-frond huts once stood. Wild date palms still grow along the west coast of Qatar. The archaeologists found fire pits, cutting tools and scrapers and a range of beautifully-made tanged arrowheads. People would have hunted game such as gazelle and onager (a species of wild ass) and all kinds of birds including ostriches and bustards. As well as fish they also caught marine mammals: dolphins and dugong.

No evidence has been found that the people who lived at Al Da'asa cultivated crops. Flint blades that look rather like sickles were probably used for gathering wild grain and grasses.

Wool was spun on a spindle made from a short stick or perhaps the stem of a reed, with a weight at the bottom called a spindlewhorl. At similar sites a little further north of Al Da'asa stone spindlewhorls have been found, showing that people were spinning thread and weaving cloth, although no textiles have survived from this time, so we do not know what sort of cloth they were making.

Around 10,000 years ago sheep and goats, which would have provided the wool, were first domesticated in the Zagros mountains of Iran and in southern Turkey. By 6,000 years ago the Neolithic people all over Arabia were keeping domesticated animals, although it may have taken longer for the camel to be domesticated than the other animals. Camels were probably first kept for their milk, wool and meat and only later used for transport.

This section through a midden in Wadi Al Debaiaan (c.5,200 BP) clearly shows the dark organic layers, containing mostly charcoal and fishbone

Stone implements from Wadi Al Debaiaan — an arrowhead, a knife and a scraper

More Ubaid sites were found near Al Khor in the 1970s, with large quantities of fish bones and stone tools and the remains of a human burial.

More recently a coastal site at Wadi Al Debaiaan, a few kilometres south of Al Zubara, was discovered. Because the sea level is now lower the site lies some distance inland , but 7,500 years ago it was located on the coast. Archaeologists have found evidence of post holes and hearths, showing that there were once a number of buildings at Wadi Al Debaiaan.

Almost 200 sherds of Ubaid pottery have been found at Wadi Al Debaiaan, plus flint tools and some fragments of obsidian, a dark glassy volcanic rock from the Taurus mountains in eastern Turkey. Wadi Al Debaiaan was one of a number of coastal Ubaid sites, which are also found in Kuwait and Saudi Arabia. These may form part of a network of trade and exchange from the Arabian Gulf along the Tigris and Euphrates rivers, and so into what is now eastern Turkey.

Two middens of waste material began to accumulate around 5,200 years ago, and are composed largely of charcoal, bone and shells. One had gradually piled up on a sandy and rocky shoreline, but the other was full of the kind of shells that are found in muddy mangrove areas. Pollen from mangrove flowers has been identified, showing that mangroves grew around the coast of Qatar a lot earlier than anyone had realised.

There are such large quantities of fish bones both at Wadi Al Debaiaan and at the Al Khor sites that it seems probable that dried fish was being exported. It may be that Mesopotamian fishermen landed at these sites to salt and dry their catch, bringing with them their precious Ubaid pots, or perhaps there was a settled population trading with them.

The site seems to have been occupied, perhaps intermittently, until around 4,500 years ago when a sudden climatic event, possibly even a tsunami, meant people had to abandon it.

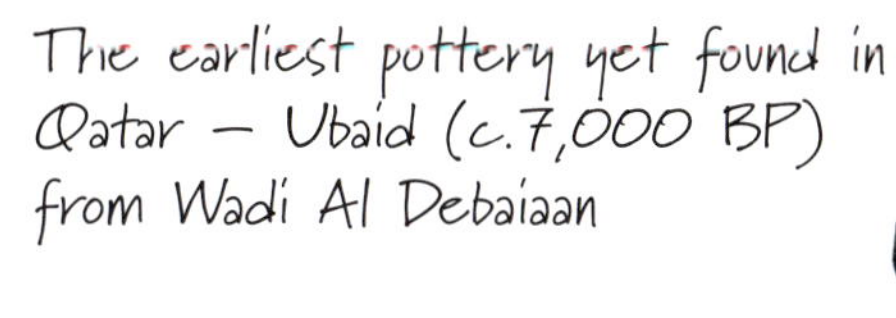

Pieces of obsidian imported from eastern Turkey, found at Wadi Al Debaiaan

The earliest pottery yet found in Qatar — Ubaid (c.7,000 BP) from Wadi Al Debaiaan

Stone pendant and shell beads from a necklace (c.7,500 BP) found at Wadi Al Debaiaan

STONE TOOLS

Thousands of years before metal was discovered, people made tools from stone, mostly from a hard, shiny stone called flint. Beautifully shaped spear and arrow heads were used for hunting and fishing, and also as weapons. Scrapers stripped fat from animal skins and the skins could then be made into leather. Sharp blades were used to cut up the carcasses of animals and to crack bones to extract the nutritious marrow. Other blades were fitted into wooden handles and used as sickles to cut plants, including wild grasses. Bulky stone axes were needed to cut down trees and split logs.

The cutting edge

Stone Age people who did not settle in one place but travelled around are known as hunter-gatherers, and the tools found in Qatar are among the most elegant and finely-made to be found anywhere. The most beautiful of them, produced in the Late Stone Age about 6,000 years ago, were fabricated by a sophisticated method known as pressure-flaking. Tiny flakes from the cutting edges were struck off to produce a razor-sharp edge or even a serrated one.

Archaeologists give stone tools names according to their shape and size, such as 'thumbnail' or 'D-shaped' scrapers and 'tanged and barbed' or 'leaf-shaped' arrowheads.

Flint in Qatar comes in many colours and was used to make a range of tools

Cooking equipment, Neolithic style! Some of the domestic tools found at Al Da'asa

The peninsula of Qatar has several deposits of fine quality flint, ranging in colour from creamy white to glossy black, and there is evidence that workshops produced tools not just for immediate use but for export. Sometimes they were made first as roughly-shaped 'blanks', which would then be finished off by a skilled craftsman at another local site or even outside Qatar. Some of these 'blanks' from Qatar have been found on sites in the United Arab Emirates.

A flint core from which pieces have been struck

An annoying loss

One day long ago a hunter was after birds in the reeds of a freshwater lake in the west of Qatar. He fired off an arrow, which missed its target and fell into the mud at the bottom of the lake. Over thousands of years, as Qatar became gradually drier, the mud solidified and turned into stone. Now the arrowhead has been found, still embedded in the rocky layer. It's like a link with the past – we can imagine how annoying it was for the hunter to lose his arrow, because we'd feel just the same in that situation.

A modern replica of an axe head

Tools for the job

Other kinds of stone were used to make implements for the preparation of food. On the site of a hunter gatherer camp at Al Da'asa archaeologists found a neat pile of useful domestic objects – limestone querns and a grinder, and a lump of coral which may have served as a grater or grinder. Whoever left them there, ready for use on their next visit to the site, never returned, and they lay there, forgotten, for thousands of years.

A selection of beautifully-made pressure-flaked arrowheads, all found in Qatar

MAKING TOOLS FROM STONE

The earliest humans started to make tools out of stone around 1.7 million years ago, in Africa. The first tools were large, clumsy hand axes, but over many thousands of years manufacturing techniques were developed and improved until some of the tools produced in Qatar during the late Stone Age, such as the delicate little arrow heads, are real works of art

Here Faisal Abdulla Al-Naimi, head of the Department of Antiquities in Qatar, demonstrates how to make a stone axe, using a thick piece of bone to knap the flint. Re-creating ancient skills like pottery manufacture, metal smelting and making stone tools is called experimental archaeology and is very important in helping us understand how our ancestors made use of whatever natural materials were available to them.

Making tools out of stone is called knapping, and the stone used in Qatar is a fine-grained rock called flint. It crops out of the limestone bedrock in two forms: round or irregularly-shaped lumps called nodules, and thin flat pieces called tabular flint. The hammers to strike the flint while tool-shaping were sometimes made of stone, but also animal horn, bone or wood. Experts can even tell by looking at a stone tool what kind of hammer was used to shape it!

Making a hand axe out of flint involves several stages

1.
First of all, the flint nodule has to be prepared by removing its outer limestone layer, the cortex. The shape of the piece of flint will, to some extent, help the knapper to decide what size and shape of tool he can make.

Faisal Abdulla Al-Naimi, head of the Department of Antiquities

2.
Then the knapper starts to prepare the surface of the flint by knocking off thin flakes with a hammer, often attached to the limestone cortex. Sometimes the stone ripples where it is struck — this is called the bulb of percussion.

3.
Once the tool has been roughly shaped, the knapper refines it by removing more flakes.

4.
Finally, he carefully removes tiny, thin flakes to reduce the thickness of the tool and create a sharp cutting edge.

COLOUR FROM THE SEA

In the bay of Al Khor lies a little island called Jazirat bin Ghannam, shaped like a fish (pictured right) and tethered to the coast by a causeway, cut at intervals to let the tide flow through to the mangrove forest on either side.

It's a peaceful place, with sandy shores and white limestone cliffs. No one lives there now, but people lived on or visited the island to hunt, or to go fishing or pearling, for over 5,000 years.

Almost three and a half thousand years ago a small factory was set up on the island to produce something more valuable even than pearls: a rich reddish-purple dye. Red is the colour of blood, of fire, of the sun and therefore of life itself, and it was seen as a symbol of power. Only kings and nobles could wear robes of this colour.

The Phoenicians, a Mediterranean people originating in Lebanon, were famous in ancient times for the production of purple dye. A Phoenician legend relates how it was discovered. A god named Melkarth was strolling along the beach one day with his sheepdog when the animal crunched on a shellfish. Noticing its jaws stained red, Melkarth realised the colour had come from the shellfish. He had purple-dyed wool woven into cloth to make a gown, which he presented to his girlfriend Tyros.

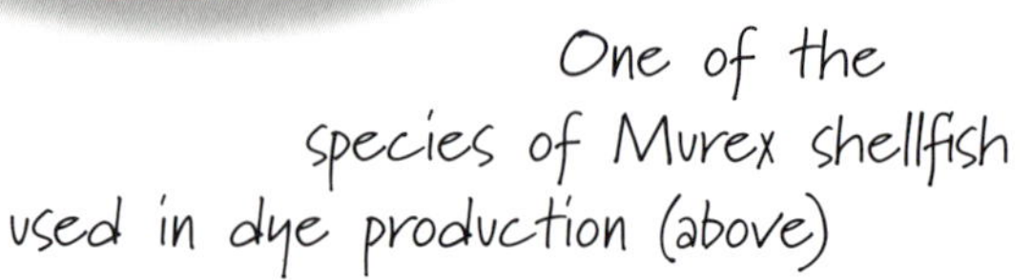

One of the species of Murex shellfish used in dye production (above)

Crushed shells from the island midden

The people making dye on the island Al Khor may have been working for the Kassites, a mountain people who had invaded and conquered part of what is now Iraq and had set up a kingdom there. To produce just a tiny quantity of dye the island workers had to find thousands of sea snails. It's been calculated that to obtain just one gramme of the pure purple colourant would require at least 10,000 snails.

To obtain the dye, the shells must be either crushed or pierced to expose a gland which gives off a slimy transparent mucus. As soon as it's exposed to light the mucus begins to change colour, first to yellow, then green, then blue and finally a shade of violet.

The glands can be smeared directly onto cloth to dye it, but the colour is rather uneven. To make a strong dye solution they can be heated gently in water, to which potash has been added to achieve alkalinity, for about a week. The smell is awful! But the result is a strong rich shade of violet which never fades.

We do not know exactly how the dye was exported, but one way of making it easily transportable is to let the glands soak into rough salt, which can then be dried. All the dye-master had to do when he wanted to dye woollen thread was to let the coloured salt dissolve in the dye bath.

If you visit the island today you can still see the rectangles of stones where the huts of the workers once stood, and the mounds of broken shells, known as middens. Archaeologists investigating the site in the 1980s found ash-filled hearths and pits, and lots of pieces of rough pottery.

The shellfish that the dye producers used all those years ago are still living in the shallow water around the island, hiding under rocks. The archaeologists estimated that the middens contained the remains of around 3 million snails!

THE MOUNDS OF THE DEAD

For thousands of years before the coming of Islam, people in Qatar were buried under cairns: mounds of rocks covering a hole dug into the ground surface, into which the dead person was placed. Sometimes these holes were cut into the limestone rock, but elsewhere they were simply hollowed out of the earth.

At the time these cairns were made, people believed that the dead could take their possessions with them into the afterlife. All over the world, ancient graves have been found to contain 'grave goods': anything that might be useful to the dead person in the next world. Clay pots of food and drink were often put beside the body. Men might be buried with their weapons, women with their jewellery. Children sometimes had their toys placed beside them in the grave. When ancient burials are excavated, these items are very helpful to archaeologists and historians because they can tell us a lot about the culture and beliefs of that period.

Groups of cairn burials are found all over Qatar, especially in the north. The neighbouring island of Bahrain once had the largest number of cairn burials in the world, spanning thousands of years and estimated to number around 100,000. Most have now been cleared away to make room for building development.

Bone does not survive well in Qatar's soil, due to the harsh conditions. Often all that is left are a few fragments, or just an outline of a skeleton where the body once rested. At Simaisma on the east coast, a cairn covered a cluster of cells in a circle described as a 'rosette burial', with but no obvious chamber in the centre. One cell contained a 'crouched' burial, where the corpse was laid on its side with knees drawn up to the chest. It appeared to be the burial of a child, with a small stone jar placed alongside the body.

A Warrior's Grave

At Al Mazrouah, north of Doha, is a group of four cairns covering burials. One contained the skeletons of crouching camels, but the grave between them had long ago been robbed and all that remained was a glass flask. There are ancient references in other parts of Arabia to the sacrifice of camels around the graves of warriors.

Above: a silver ring (left) and one made of seashell (right), both from Umm Al Maa

Below: beads and pierced shells from Umm Al Maa

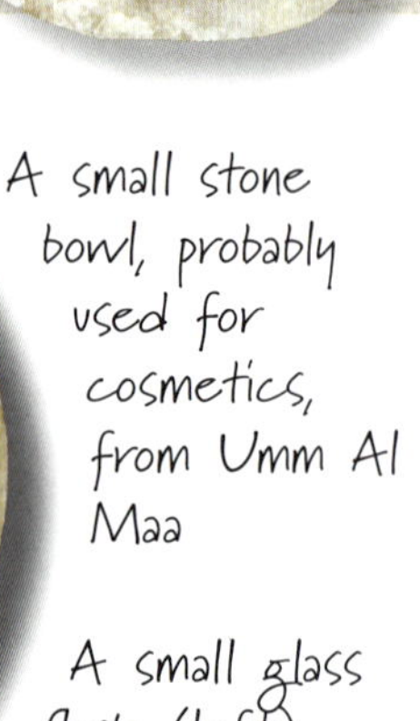

A small stone bowl, probably used for cosmetics, from Umm Al Maa

A small glass flask (left) from Al Mazrouah

The cairns may perhaps date to the Iron Age as some objects made of iron were found in the grave. One was certainly the grave of a warrior: a male human skeleton lay beside an iron sword and a bundle of iron arrowheads. The second burial was of a man with an iron arrowhead beside his waist and another embedded in a bone in his forearm! Who were he and his tribe fighting? No one knows.

An arm bone with an arrowhead embedded in it from Al Mazrouah

Cairns at Umm Al Maa and at Lisha on the north-west coast of Qatar have also been been dated to the Iron Age, spanning a period roughly 2300 to 1700 BP. Round or oval pits were dug into the rock through a thin surface layer of dark brown sand, and low walls were built around the edges of the pits with three or four larger stone blocks.

The bodies were placed either in a sitting position or laid on their side in the pits, together with grave goods. Each pit was then covered with a layer of flat capstones of beach rock, known as *farush* in Arabic. Sand layers were piled above these and then the whole thing was covered with closely piled stones.

A stone pendant from Umm Al Maa (left)

More than 40 iron arrowheads like these were buried with a warrior at Al Mazrouah

Despite these efforts to let the dead rest in peace, about two-thirds of all the burials examined so far by archaeologists had been robbed in antiquity, sometimes not long after the burials had taken place. The bones were roughly piled on one side by the robbers as they searched for anything worth looting. So mostly, all that remains of the grave goods are broken scraps.

Burial at Lisha, with an iron sword (below) beside the skeleton

Sometimes fragments of useful items remain, such as bronze and copper bowls and grinding stones, painted and glazed pottery and glass vessels. Perhaps these were smashed by the robbers as they scrabbled to find more precious items. Beads of glass and a white and brown striped and polished stone called sardonyx came, like the pottery, from outside Qatar and show that the people were engaged in trading. Men were buried with iron swords and knives, which must have been highly valued by their owners, but usually all that remain of these now are small rusted splinters.

ROCK CARVINGS

Scattered round the the coasts of Qatar are low coastal limestone hills. A number of these feature strange carvings on the surface of the soft rock. Recently, some experts on dating rock carvings have suggested that it is unlikely that any are older than a few hundred years at the most. But others are convinced that at least some of the carvings may be very much older than this.

The best-known rocks with carvings are at Jabal al Jassasiya and Fuwairit on the east coast, and at Fraiha in the north-west. There are even some right in the middle of Doha, in a park beside the Corniche!

Rock carvings are known as 'petroglyphs', and all the carved rocks in Qatar have examples of 'cup marks'. Some of these small, circular depressions are single; others are massed together in a variety of formations: one, two, three or four lines of cups. Some lines are straight and others are curved, or the holes are clustered together in 'rosettes' with anything from six to sixteen cups surrounding a larger central depression.

Gaming boards?

Some archaeologists think that the double rows of cup marks were used for playing a very ancient game, known all over the world, where two opponents drop odd and even numbers of counters into the holes. But some of the rows of holes are on slopes where counters would have fallen out. And some are too small to hold anything bigger than grains of rice. What were they really for? No one knows for sure, and your guess is as good as anyone's.

Making your mark

At several sites foot marks are carved into the rock, sometimes just a simple narrow oval or pair of oval shapes. Others are complete with toes! The making of foot and hand marks on rock and the painting of hand prints in caves is very ancient. Experts have dated hand prints in a cave in southern France to 27,000 BP.

Limestone hills

Rosette formation of cup marks (above) and a double row of cup marks at Jabal al Jassasiya (below)

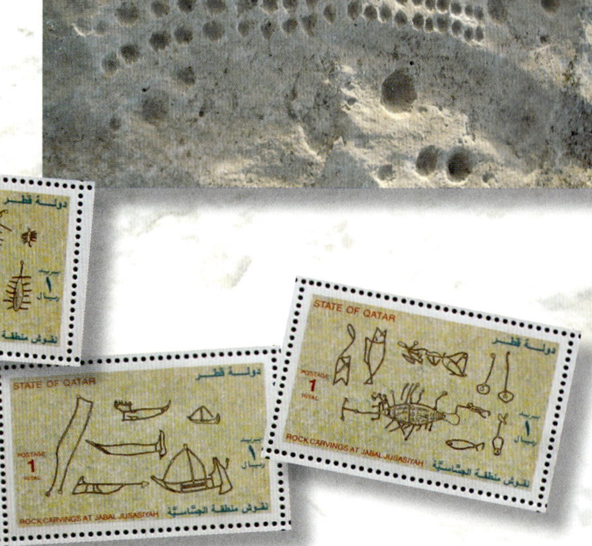

Qatar postage stamps from 1995, featuring rock carvings

Sailing the Gulf

The most interesting carvings are of boats, and the finest are at Jabal al Jassasiya. Some show a bird's-eye view of a ship from above. Others are very different; they are linear drawings, as if you are looking at the ship from the side.

The boats seen from above are lozenge-shaped and have rows of oars. They seem to crawl over the rock like scorpions. Such boats were steered with a long oar at one end, not with a rudder like modern boats. Some trail long ropes attached either to a traditional triangular stone anchor or to a metal anchor. Metal anchors were first used in the Gulf about 700 years ago.

On some of the boats the oars are not parallel, as they would have to be when used for rowing, but are all pointing in different directions. This is how they would have looked when the boats were anchored out on the pearl banks and the oars were left in place for the divers to cling to and rest each time they came up.

On one group of rocks are 17 detailed carvings, in which the lines have been pecked out using a pointed metal tool and a hammer. They are interesting because of the number of recognisable types of sailing vessels. The artists were careful to include the details that would enable a ship to be easily identified. One, a 'battil', has the characteristic round projection at the bow and a high stern. *Battils* were large, fast vessels, extensively employed in the pearling fleets but also useful as warships. Another illustration may be of a 'baqqarah', with a projecting frame at the stern. The decorated stern post has a lantern holder. The hulls of both *battil* and *baqqarah* are divided by vertical lines to indicate the size and loading capacity of the ship – just the sort of information which would have been important to a sea-faring people. One of the line-drawn boats has a row of small windows at the stern, a feature of the Portuguese ships which first appeared in the Gulf 600 years ago and influenced the designs of the local boat builders.

Ships held a powerful role in the beliefs of ancient peoples, who saw them as a symbolic means of transit from this world to the next. Both Babylonians and ancient Egyptians believed that the dead reached the afterworld upon a ship. Greek myths spoke of the ferryman Charon who carried the souls of the dead across the river Styx to the underworld. It may be that the oldest of the ship carvings are echoes of a folk memory reaching far back into pre-historic times.

THE GOLDEN AGE

The golden age of Arab trade and culture began in 762 CE when the Abbasid caliphs moved the capital of the Arab Empire from Damascus to Baghdad.

They took their name from an uncle of the Prophet Muhammed called Abbas ibn 'Abd al-Muttalib, from whom they were descended. Bahgdad became a centre for science, medicine and education. Scholars translated thousands of books from around the world into Arabic and Persian, many of them Greek and Latin texts that would otherwise have been lost. Astronomers, poets, philosophers, medical scientists and engineers all made Baghdad their home.

The port of Basra was founded, and from it ships sailed all over the known world. Trade with China began, and luxury goods like tea, spices, perfume, silk, paper and fine ceramics were carried by great ocean-going dhows along the long sea route from the South China Sea and up through the Arabian Gulf to Basra. Their captains navigated with astonishing accuracy, using a *kamal*, a simple wood and string device to determine their latitude by measuring the altitude of stars above the horizon.

*Battil*s were typical of the trading ships of the time. They carried two masts with large square sails, rather than the triangular 'lateen' sails typical of the Gulf ships of later years, and were built of long planks tightly stitched together with rope made of coconut fibre. Under the stitching was a layer of coconut fibre wadding, saturated with fish oil to make it water-resistant. The outside of the hull was then further waterproofed with a mixture of chalk, resin and fish oil.

A new invention around this time was a single central rudder at the stern, which gradually began to replace the two long steering oars which had been in use for centuries.

Exports such as cotton and woollen cloth, pearls and all kinds of metal objects flowed the other way. This was the age of the merchant-adventurer Sindbad the Sailor, who boasted that he could turn a cargo worth 3,000 silver coins into one worth 10,000 golden coins! The fantastic stories about him were first written down at this time in the famous *Tales of the Arabian Nights*.

Above: the 'Jewel of Muscat', a replica built in Oman in 2010 of a 9th century trading ship

Left: a kamal used for measuring latitude

The people living in Qatar, too, had a part in the trade and wealth of this glorious age of trade and scientific discovery. The settlement of Murwab, a few kilometres from the coast in the north-west, dates to the time of the Abbasids, and has the oldest forts and mosques found anywhere in the peninsula. It lies in a depression which was famous among the nomadic bedu people for the vegetation which sprang up after rain. Nothing was written down at the time about the daily lives of people in Qatar, so we have to rely on what archaeologists have discovered to help us imagine what it must have been like to be around in such an exciting time. There are the remains of more than 200 small stone-built houses at Murwab, but many more people would have lived on the outskirts of the settlement in temporary accommodation such as tents and palm-leaf huts.

The two small forts were square. One was built on the ruins of the other, which had been destroyed by fire. They were constructed of limestone blocks, plastered on both sides, with a tower on each corner, a narrow entrance and a deep well in the courtyard. The fort was the home of the chief of the tribe, and in times of danger people would crowd into the courtyard.

The mosques are very small too, but people would have gathered for prayers on the open ground beside them. More than 200 houses lie along a street running east to west. They are small and rectangular and were probably roofed with beams of wood from palm trees and woven leafy matting. Some had plastered floors, and in one of them was a pile of pearl oyster shells and some diving weights, showing that the people were fishing for pearls. There are also some date presses where sacks of dates could be weighted and left to produce delicious, nourishing date syrup called *dibs*. A date press consists of a rectangular or square area deeply

grooved with parallel channels, onto which sacks of dates were piled. The weight compressed the dates and caused a sweet, sticky syrup to ooze out, which then trickled down the channels to where a large jar was sunk into the ground.

It is not just the houses which tell us how relatively well-off were the people of Murwab, but the remnants of their possessions. Everywhere the sandy ground sparkles with bits of fine coloured glass and ceramics. Finds include blue glazed pottery from Basra, and cream and green glazed ceramics from Iran and what is now Uzbekistan. Other objects such as a little model of a lion and a lamp, both made of bronze, show the variety of goods imported through Basra.

The Golden Age in Qatar did not last long. After about a century of occupation Murwab was abandoned, probably because of rebellions against the Abbasids in the region, which may have disrupted trade or even caused some populations in the area to move altogether. For over a thousand years the ruins lay silent and deserted. The bedu camped among them from time to time, and left fragments of pottery which can be dated, but until the archaeologists arrived with their spades and trowels the name of Murwab was almost lost in the mists of time.

Objects found at Murwab: copper-glazed water jars, a bronze lamp, a small bronze lion, and a lamp made of a soft stone called steatite

NOMADS OF THE DESERT

For thousands of years the people of Qatar lived in villages around the coast, where they engaged in fishing and pearling and the growing of dates and other produce. But there were other people in Qatar, too, the nomadic bedu. They had no settled home and travelled with their flocks of camels, sheep and goats wherever there was good rainfall and they could find pasture for their animals.

Like all nomads, the bedu moved lightly on the land, and today there are few traces remaining of a way of life that continued unbroken for many centuries until they finally chose to settle in villages in the 1950s and 1960s, where they could get access to clean water and electricity and, most importantly, good health care and education for the children. Today, many of their descendants live in Doha.

Young girls (pictured in south Qatar in 1959) sit spinning goats' wool and plaiting their hair

Sometimes you may come across rings of stones in the desert, which show where tents were pitched, or carvings on rocks. But little else is left to show where the bedu once lived in their low black tents, sometimes for many months, before packing up and moving on.

When moving camp sites, the travellers found their way over long distances not with any navigational aids as we do today, but by using their powers of observation to the full, noting every slight change in plant life and sand dune, as they went along. Many places in Qatar are named after plants, or after unusually shaped rocks, or after the ripples made by the wind on a dune. These place names were known to everyone in Qatar. People did not need directions: if a place was mentioned by name they'd know where it was.

The bedu lived on milk and meat from their animals, and some tribes owned date plantations. They hunted for wild game, including migrating birds such bustards and stone curlews, and also hares. The hunters used falcons and saluki dogs, and trapped small rodents and lizards. Many of the desert plants were either edible or could be used for firewood or the making of medicines or soap, and even for the manufacture of gunpowder! Women made cosmetics from desert plants. Rice,

Loading the camels at a camp at Oqlat Al Manaseet, south Qatar, in 1959

sugar, tea and coffee were traded for with the settled people of the towns.

Tent cloth of dark brown goat's hair with cream-coloured stripes was woven on a loom. The name for a tent in Arabic, *beit sha'ar,* means 'house of hair'. Sheepswool was preferred for making items like saddle bags, blankets and woven carpets. Camels were essential to the way of life of the nomads. They were known as *Ata Allah,* the Gift of God. Camels provided everything from milk to meat and hair for weaving. Camel leather was made into a whole range of useful articles: hanging cradles for babies, saddles, water scoops, bags and plaited ropes. Camel hair was woven into bags and blankets, or netted with a needle into rather prickly socks which were worn in very hot or very cold weather.

The leaves of date palms were useful materials for making mats, baskets, fans and sweeping brushes. You can still see these articles on sale today in the *souqs.* Woven huts made from palm leaf ribs and leaves were known as *barasti,* and some tribes preferred these to tents.

Medicines for all kinds of ailments were made from plants and the bark or leaves of trees. Healers also practised cauterisation, applying a red-hot iron rod to the afflicted area. This drastic treatment was popular with pearl divers, who often suffered from aches and pains resulting from the physical stress of their work.

Some bedu worked at pearl fishing during the spring and summer months. Then in the winter they returned to their families and travelled with their camels.

It was often hard to find enough water for the needs of both people and animals, and in the very hottest months some tribes took their camels across to Bahrain, which had a constant supply of spring water. Water was carried in containers made of leather, but when motorised vehicles came to Qatar the inner tubes of tyres proved useful for transporting water. When filled they looked like giant black sausages!

Once money from the export of oil started to flow into the country, there was no need to continue a lifestyle which, although free from the hustle and bustle of city life, was often very hard. One by one the families settled in houses built for them by the government, and by the 1970s the ancient nomadic wandering life had disappeared forever.

Preparing to move on from their camp at Oqlat Al Manaseet, south Qatar, in 1959, and (below) setting forth for new pastures

A storage bag made by a weaver from the Dawasir tribe

SEEKING THE ANGELS' TEARDROPS

Archaeologists have found pearls, some of them drilled with holes, on sites dating back more than 7,000 years in Kuwait and the United Arab Emirates. One of the oldest pieces of literature in the world, the *Epic of Gilgamesh* from Mesopotamia, describes how the hero Gilgamesh dived with weights to look for a treasure on the bottom of the sea.

Pearls in the Arabian Gulf are found in oysters. Legends said that when it rained the oysters rose to the surface and opened their shells to receive the drops of rain which turned into pearls. Other stories held that they formed when lightning struck the sea, or were the teardrops of angels!

Until recently people thought that pearls formed around grains of sand which got inside the shell and irritated the oyster. But now we know that they form when the outer edge of the oyster's flesh is injured, usually by an intruding parasitic worm. This causes cells to break loose and become trapped deep inside the shellfish, where they grow into a pearl.

Pearling in Qatar was an important source of income because, until the discovery of oil in 1939, followed by the first oil export on 31 December 1949, the country had few natural resources. A hundred years ago, 70,000 men in the Arabian Gulf were engaged in pearl diving, and in Qatar almost all able-bodied men took part. We know a lot about how the pearling season was organised, and about the methods of diving, which can't have changed much for thousands of years.

The pearling season was divided into three:
- a 40-day 'cold dive' period which began in April;
- followed by a long stint which lasted from May to the end of September. All the ships had to sail together to the areas where the oysters grew, known as pearl banks, and return at the same time. It must have been a wonderful and impressive sight when a fleet of a hundred or more pearling dhows headed out from a harbour.
- Finally, there was a short period, of about three weeks, usually on pearl banks nearer the coast.

Top: a pearl oyster 'Pinctada radiata' with pearl, from the Arabian Gulf; above: opening pearl oysters on board a boat in 1960

Singing songs to the beat of a drum helped divers forget the dangers of their work

Each boat carried anything between 30 and 100 men. The captain was always someone with years of experience, who could locate the best pearl beds without using maps, by observing the currents and the state of the sea surface. Besides the divers there were the pullers, whose job it was to wait for a signal from the divers that they were ready to come up and quickly haul them to the surface. An important member of the crew was the singer, who sang, clapped and beat out a rhythm on a drum to cheer the men while they were working and distract them from their dangerous working conditions.

Each morning the men opened and searched the oysters gathered the day before and then threw the shells overboard. Any pearls found were held between their toes, to be collected by the captain. Then they prepared for the first dive by fixing pincers of turtleshell to their noses, putting on a cotton suit to protect them against jellyfish stings, and leather finger stalls to prevent scratches from the rough shells of the oysters. When he was ready, each diver placed his foot in a loop of rope to which stone or lead weights were attached, and dropped to the sea bed. He was attached to a second, thinner rope and used a knife to prise the shellfish from the rocks, collecting them in a net bag slung round his neck. When he could not hold his breath any longer, up he came for a short rest as he clung to an oar before diving again. Some men made more than 50 dives a day.

Sometimes the pearl merchants visited the pearling fleet to bargain directly with the captains for the pearls, but on other occasions dealers and the owners of the boats would gather as soon as the fleet anchored in port, and fierce bargaining took place for the season's precious haul of 'jewels from the sea'. India was the main market for Gulf pearls, but others found their way to Europe and America.

Fishing for pearls may sound romantic, but in fact it was a very hard and dangerous way to make a living. Divers sometimes went blind or deaf when quite young, and there was the constant fear of attacks by sharks and stingrays, or infected injuries from being scraped against rocks or coral. Divers had to borrow money before each voyage to feed their families while they were away, and most never got free of debt. When oil production began in Qatar in the early 1950s, the last of the divers were glad to exchange their harsh life for better-paid jobs in the oil industry.

A pearl merchant's red cloth bag, called a 'dasta', containing graded sieves, scales, a small scoop, a bag of agate weights, and a book used to calculate the value of pearls in relation to their weight

A turtleshell noseclip used by divers

A stone diving weight

An agate weight for weighing pearls

Above: a pearling boat called a 'jalbut' leaving Doha port in 1960

Below: divers about to descend to the seabed, 1960

AL ZUBARA

The old city of Al Zubara lies on the north-west coast of Qatar. For many years it lay empty and deserted, its walls crumbling into mounds of sandy rubble littered with fragments of green-glazed water jars, earthenware cooking pots and pieces of Chinese glazed porcelain. But long ago it was a hive of busy activity, its streets crowded with people and its harbour full of fishing and pearling boats and trading ships carrying cargoes of luxury goods to the settlement.

Al Zubara town

Now Al Zubara has come to life again, as a team of archaeologists uncovers the remains of the buildings and reveals details of the daily lives of the people in this once thriving port. Al Zubara is the best example in the Arabian Gulf of a pearl fishing and trading port dating from before the modern oil era. Because it was abandoned more than a century ago, the street plan and the remains of the buildings have remained undisturbed.

The town was laid out according to a plan, with narrow lanes running down to the sea. Houses were built of beach rock, or from limestone quarried at Fraiha, a short distance to the north of the city. Some people lived in temporary accommodation – tents, or *barasti* huts constructed of woven palm leaves. A *souq* with rows of little shops stood near the shoreline, and there was a small industrial complex where metal was smelted in crucibles .

The former police post at Al Zubara, built in 1937

During the 18th and 19th centuries Al Zubara held an important position as a trading centre, linking sea routes that ran both north and south along the coasts of the Arabian Gulf. Some of the coins and trading tokens found at Al Zubara came from Persia, India, Turkey, Zanzibar and British-ruled East Africa, showing how widespread was the trade.

The people of Al Zubara enjoyed a comparatively wealthy lifestyle, and their wealth had to be protected from raiders. A fort was built in 1768 to guard the town, and a wall with round towers at intervals surrounded the settlement. But in spite of these precautions the town was attacked on several occasions. After 1811, when Al Zubara was

A section through the midden next to a tower of the fortified 'palace' compound

partly burnt to the ground by forces from the Sultanate of Muscat, the town was resettled but shrank to a third of its former size. Bowls and cups of blue and white Chinese porcelain, specially made for export, were imported in huge quantities into Al Zubara and other smaller towns along the coast. Cooking pots from Julfar in what is now the United Arab Emirates were made of coarse orange or grey pottery. Water and rice was stored in large jars imported from Bahrain or Iran. A number of small clay tobacco pipe bowls, some of them attractively patterned, show that tobacco was one of the imports enjoyed by the inhabitants.

There are many date presses, where sacks of dates were piled up to allow *dibs*, the sweet sticky juice that oozes from the compressed dates, to trickle down narrow channels into collecting jars.

A trading token from Bavaria in southern Germany, c. 1800

An engraving of a sailing dhow on wall plaster

One complex of fortified buildings has been nicknamed 'the palace' by archaeologists. It is likely to have been the home of the ruling family of the town, and was subdivided into a number of courtyards, screened from the gaze of visitors by walls. Some of the houses had two storeys. There were several bathrooms, and decorated panels of gypsum plaster on the walls.

Coral beads

Recently a large wall panel was discovered with a fine engraving of a trading or pearling dhow, similar in style to some of those on the petroglyph site at Jabal al Jassasiya. Such ships would have been an everyday sight for the people of Al Zubara.

Near the palace is a midden – a rubbish heap. Middens are like gold mines for archaeologists. Examining their contents, often under a microscope, can reveal a mass of detail about the daily lifestyles of the people. This midden contains evidence, in the form of animal bones, that the people of the palace ate meat more frequently than the other inhabitants of Al Zubara, who relied on fish as their main source of protein, another indication that they were well off.

A decorated terracotta tobacco pipe bowl from Turkey

A small jar containing a collection of beads, some of semi-precious stones

The biggest problem for the people of Al Zubara was obtaining enough fresh water. It had to be brought from wells some distance inland, and even then the fresh water may have had to be scooped off a layer of salty water underneath. It seems probable that the reason the settlement was eventually abandoned at the beginning of the 20th century was the failure of the water supply.

A bronze spoon

A LOST SETTLEMENT AND AN ANCIENT FORT

A cannonball found embedded in the wall of the fort at Al Rubaiqa

The coastline of Qatar is dotted with the remains of small villages and the ruins of larger towns such as Al Zubara on the west coast and Al Huwaila in the east. Pearl fishing, trading and fishing provided a livelihood for the coast dwellers. They built their houses with slabs of 'beach rock' from the sea.

A 6 cm-high chess piece from Al Rubaiqa

On a lonely stretch of coastline at Ras Eshariq, the small cape which juts out into the sea south of Al Zubara, a scatter of stones caught the eye of archaeologists exploring the area. There was little to show on the sandy surface – just a few rocks and some low, wind-weathered mounds. But to archaeologists the signs indicated that there was something interesting below the surface.

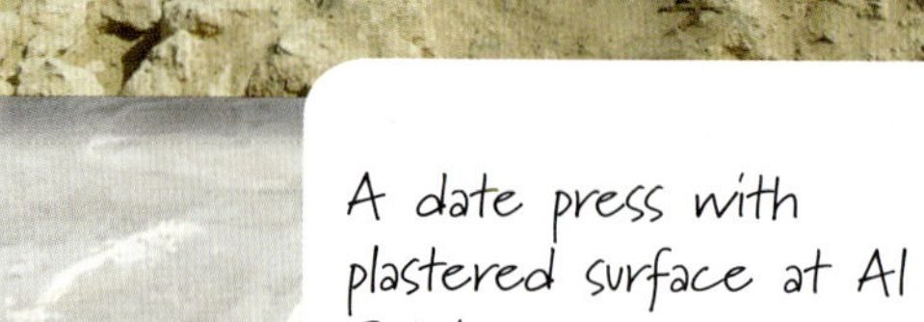

They had discovered a little settlement named Al Rubaiqa. As they excavated, the archaeologists noticed a curious thing: the inhabitants were not fishermen, nor were they fishing for pearls. So why did they choose to live on the coast? The answer may lie in Al Rubaiqa's proximity to deep water, which allowed large ships to approach the land. Another clue is the number of date presses.

A date press with plastered surface at Al Rubaiqa

What's going on?

Something odd about the Al Rubaiqa date presses is that no two are alike. Some are coated with fine white gypsum plaster, others are not. Some have pits for two collecting jars, not one. One press has an extraordinary twisted maze of collecting channels.

The base of a 19th century Persian fritware bowl

If the inhabitants were exporting date syrup, where were the date plantations? It may be that the dates were imported from the huge oasis at Al-Hasa in Saudi Arabia. Al Rubaiqa may have been a sort of processing and storage facility for nomadic tribes to stock up before wandering the deserts.

Middens containing ash and fragments of pottery and animal bone indicate a long period of occupation for Al Rubaiqa. Some of the pottery was made around 500 years ago at Julfar in the northern Emirates. Archaeologists also found fragments of glazed pottery from China and Burma and pottery from Iraq and Iran.

Lost and found

In addition to houses, there was a walled area with a single corner tower facing landwards, which is believed to be a fort. Embedded in the walls of this 'fort' was a large cannon ball, with another nearby on the ground! History records many instances of attack along this stretch of coast in the 18th and 19th centuries – life was not always peaceful in Al Rubaiqa. This particular attack appears to have taken place in the 1890s. Burnt roofing timbers on top of everyday objects suggest the fires occurred suddenly while the buildings were still occupied.

Someone hastily stuffed a cotton bag containing nineteen Indian silver rupees into a crevice in the wall of a mosque. But whoever hid their savings never returned to recover them. The inhabitants fled, and Al Rubaiqa was left to the drifting sand.

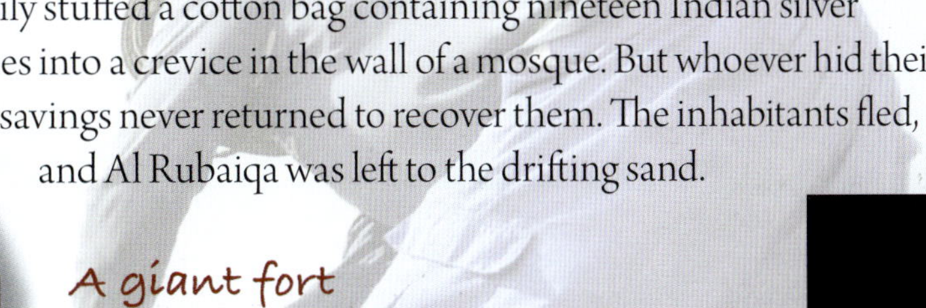

A silver rupee from India with the date 1879

A giant fort

Near the tip of the Qatar peninsula are the ruins of an impressively large fort, Qalaat Al Ruwaida, and the remains of a village and two cemeteries. The site covers more than two kilometres of the coast beside a shallow bay.

Lots of potsherds give clues to the date of occupation. Coarse cooking wares came from the Emirates and Bahrain, and fine glazed table wares from Persia. From China and South East Asia came porcelain manufactured specially for export, almost all dating from before 1750 CE. Besides the pottery the archaeologists found beads made of carnelian, bits of glass bangles, fragments of copper, and bowls made of a soft stone called chlorite schist.

The fort is square and appears to have been occupied between four hundred and two hundred years ago. The original fort was constructed with four corner towers; later it was enlarged northwards by building an enclosure wall without towers. Later still it was expanded by more enclosures to the west and south-east. Between the fort and the sea is a mosque which was rebuilt several times.

A shipping channel was dredged in the bay, and near the entrance to the fort is a building which probably served as a merchants' warehouse. Rich pearl banks lie less than ten kilometres distant, and the remains of stone fish traps show that there was a thriving fishing industry. For centuries fish was an important part of the diet of Qatari people and more than 400 fish traps still lie around the coastline.

The site was abandoned around 200 years ago. There were severe cholera epidemics around this time and it may be that so many people died that a large settlement like Al Ruwaida could no longer keep going. Silence descended on the settlement, broken only by the haunting calls of sea birds, until the archaeologists arrived.

A red granite mortar from Al Ruwaida

A selection of ceramic sherds made in China, Europe and Persia (Iran) found at Al Rubaiqa and Al Ruwaida

CONSERVATION OF ARCHAEOLOGICAL FINDS

Once an object has been excavated by archaeologists it has to be treated to ensure it doesn't fall apart or crumble away. Sometimes all the object needs is a little gentle cleaning, but often the work can take months, or even many years, before it can be put on display in a museum.

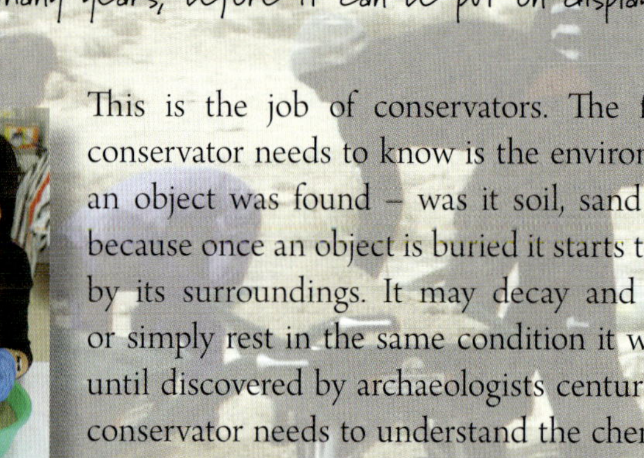

A conservator at work

This is the job of conservators. The first thing a conservator needs to know is the environment where an object was found – was it soil, sand or water? – because once an object is buried it starts to be affected by its surroundings. It may decay and disintegrate, or simply rest in the same condition it was always in until discovered by archaeologists centuries later. The conservator needs to understand the chemistry of the soil as well as deciding what material the object was made from. Materials like metal, textiles, glass, wood and leather all react differently to the type of soil in which they were buried.

Once the conservator has this information, they can decide what treatment will best ensure the survival of the object. They also need to understand how the material will react when it becomes exposed to 21st-century pollution. This is particularly important, as the effects on an object can be almost immediate and the damage caused irreparable.

The fragile remains of a pearl merchant's box at Al Zubara are excavated inside a block of soil (above), and the box after conservation in the laboratory (below)

Come at once!

Sometimes conservators get urgent calls from archaeologists to come to a site and carry out immediate conservation on an object that is too fragile to be excavated. These are usually organic objects like textiles, wood and bone, and sometimes metal, especially iron. In these cases the object has to be very carefully excavated inside the block of soil surrounding it, and conveyed to the laboratory so work can begin.

Keep it wet

Objects made of wood are sometimes found underwater or in waterlogged soil – soil that is very wet. When wood has sat in water for hundreds of years, it starts to break down, but it keeps its original shape because the water replaces the decayed material. Once excavated, if it is allowed to dry out the wood will shrink and distort and the original shape will be lost forever. To prevent this, the water must be replaced by another, more stable, material before it has time to dry.

The first thing that must happen when a waterlogged object of wood is excavated is to make sure that it does not dry out, so it is either kept submerged in a tank of water or sprayed with water. The water is replaced by a liquid form of a wax-like material called PEG